You Can Write Using Good Grammar

Jennifer Rozines Roy

Enslow Publishers, Inc.

40 Industrial Road
Box 398
Berkeley Heights, NJ 07922
USA

PO Box 38
Aldershot
Hants GU12 6BP
UK

http://www.enslow.com

Library of Congress Cataloging-in-Publication Data

Roy, Jennifer Rozines, 1967–
    You can write using good grammar / Jennifer Rozines Roy.
      v. cm. — (You can write)
    Includes bibliographical references (p.) and index.
    Contents: Why learn grammar? — Parts of speech — Sentences and
paragraphs — Using parts of speech — Punctuation, proofreading, and
other word forms — Common grammar goofs.
    ISBN 0-7660-2084-3
    1. English language—Grammar—Juvenile literature. 2. English
language—Composition and exercises—Juvenile literature. [1. English
language—Grammar. 2. English language—Composition and exercises.]
I. Title. II. Series.
   PE1112.R69 2004
   428.2—dc21
                                    2002156035

Printed in the United States of America

10 9 8 7 6 5 4 3 2 1

To Our Readers: We have done our best to make sure all Internet Addresses in this book were active and appropriate when we went to press. However, the author and the publisher have no control over and assume no liability for the material available on those Internet sites or on other Web sites they may link to. Any comments or suggestions can be sent by e-mail to comments@enslow.com or to the address on the back cover.

Illustration Credits: Enslow Publishers, Inc.

Cover Illustration: Enslow Publishers, Inc.

Table of Contents

Why Worry About Grammar?

This book can help you learn to write with great grammar. That's awesome! Why, you ask? Why not just write whatever I feel and not worry about a bunch of nitpicky rules? Well, your writing says a lot about who you are. What if you have something great to say, but other people don't understand what you mean because you didn't say it right? Or what if all they notice are the embarrassing mistakes you made? Not to worry—help is on the way.

Good grammar can help you share your ideas and opinions with others. Good grammar makes it easier for other people to understand what you are saying. You'll be more likely to say what you actually mean, and other people will be more likely to take you seriously. Good grammar can help you get good grades, express your feelings better, earn more respect from others, ace job interviews and college applications, give a great speech, help write new laws—the sky's the limit!

Good grammar? Big deal, why should I care?

In addition to reading this book, here are some things you can try to keep your grammar muscles in good shape:

- At school, ask your teacher to divide your class into "grammar groups." Take turns checking each other's papers for grammar errors before you hand them in. At home, ask a parent or an older brother or sister to give you a hand.

- Make up sayings or rhymes to help you remember grammar rules. Maybe you can share them with your class for extra credit.

- Find grammar mistakes in newspapers, books, and magazines. Bring them to class and discuss why they're wrong—and how to fix them.

- Look in other guides to grammar and writing. No one book can "do it all." Most good writers keep a few good guidebooks close by to refer to.

- Read out loud. You'll start to hear what great grammar sounds like, and soon your own writing and speaking will sound better, too!

Good luck—and have fun!

I didn't realize grammar was so fascinating! Get me into the grammar groove!

Chapter One
Parts of Speech: The Building Blocks of Good Grammar

Words, of course, make up our speech and our writing. In grammar, words are classified into different types, or **parts of speech**. The main parts of speech include nouns, pronouns, verbs, adjectives, adverbs, prepositions, conjunctions, and interjections. Each has a purpose. Nouns identify people, places, and things. Verbs show action. Adjectives describe. Sound confusing? Don't worry, you'll get a quick review of all of them in this chapter.

Nouns

A **noun** is a word used to name or identify a person, place, or thing. Nouns may name concrete things you can see or touch as well as abstract things like thoughts, feelings, or ideas. Common nouns identify things you can talk about in a general sense, like *city* or *pet* or *store* or *pride.* Proper nouns include the names of specific people, places, or things, like *Mary* or the *Yankees* or *Washington, D.C.,* or *Buddhism.* Proper nouns are capitalized.

Singular and Plural Nouns

Singular nouns refer to one person, place, or thing. Plural nouns refer to more than one. Most nouns can be made plural by adding an -s to the end. Usually, if the noun ends in -ch, -sh, -s, -x, or -z, add -es. If it ends in a consonant plus -y, change the -y to -i and add -es.

pack → packs   ski → skis

switch → switches   baby → babies

When a proper name or family name is made plural, you almost always simply add an -s. But if it ends in an *s* or *z* sound, add -es.

more than one person named Kelly → Kellys

the Smith family → the Smiths

more than one person named Charles → Charleses

the Rodriguez family → the Rodriguezes

Several nouns have irregular plural forms, which means normal rules don't apply. Some examples include:

man → men   mouse → mice

person → people   deer → deer

You may already be familiar with many irregular plural nouns. It may help to memorize the spelling of some of the more common ones, or use your dictionary if you are not sure. The entry for the singular form of a noun will usually include the plural form as well if it is considered irregular.

Possessive Nouns

The possessive form of a noun shows ownership. Adding an apostrophe plus -s will make most nouns possessive:

the chair that Carl owns = Carl's chair
the choices the women make = the women's choices

However, a plural noun that already ends in -s can be made possessive simply by adding an apostrophe:

the truck that belongs to the workers =
the workers' truck

For singular nouns that end in -s, some people recommend adding the normal apostrophe plus -s, while others feel you can simply add the apostrophe—especially if adding a second -s would make the pronunciation awkward or difficult:

the house owned by Charles =
Charles's house   OR   Charles' house

Pronouns

Pronouns are words that can be used in place of nouns. They allow a writer or speaker to refer to the person, place, or thing being discussed without having to use the same noun over and over again.

You can use a pronoun in place of a noun if that noun has already been used at least once in the same sentence or in one right before it. The noun a pronoun refers to is called the **antecedent** (*ante-* means before). It should be absolutely clear which noun the pronoun refers to. In each of the following examples, the pronoun *he* clearly refers to the noun *Simon*:

When Simon came home, he fed the puppy.
Simon came home. He fed the puppy.

But look at this example:

> After Simon fed the puppy, he fell asleep.

Who fell asleep, Simon or the puppy? It would help to rephrase the sentence, depending on what is meant:

> After feeding the puppy, Simon fell asleep.
>
> OR
>
> After Simon fed the puppy, the puppy fell asleep.

There are many different kinds of pronouns, and different forms to use depending on what you are trying to say. For example, personal pronouns such as *I*, *she*, *his*, *it*, *them*, *we*, and *yourselves* refer to specific people, places, or things. Indefinite pronouns such as *anyone*, *somebody*, *nothing*, *no one*, and *anywhere* refer to people, places, or things in general; they are not restricted to specific or definite people, places, or things.

Demonstrative pronouns show, or demonstrate, that one thing or group of things in particular is being referred to rather than another. They include *this*, *that*, *these*, and *those,* as in "*These* are faster than *those.*" Interrogative pronouns, such as *who*, *where*, *how*, and *why*, help ask questions. They represent something that is unknown: "*Who* ate my sandwich?" When pronouns such as *who* or *that* are used to help identify something more clearly or show its relationship to something else, they are considered relative pronouns: "The dog *that* just ran outside made a huge mess!"

You will learn more about pronouns and how to use them correctly in Chapter 3.

Verbs

Verbs identify the action in a sentence or describe a state of being. Verbs such as *sing* or *run* describe actions.

Verbs such as *be* or *seem* describe states of being. Some verbs might do either, depending on what is meant:

> The girl looks at the car.   *looks = action*
> The girl looks happy.   *looks = state of being*
>
> Some action verbs: *read, dance, grin*
> Some state-of-being verbs: *be, have, seem*

You will learn more about verbs and how to use them correctly in Chapter 3.

Adjectives

Adjectives are modifiers that describe nouns or pronouns. Adjectives can describe color, taste, scent, sight, touch, quality, speed, height, depth, feelings, and lots of other qualities. Adjectives add information and interest to your sentences. For example, which of these dogs would you rather play with?

> The dog wore a collar.
> The funny dog wore a ruffled, blue, polka-dotted collar.

There are different kinds of adjectives, including descriptive, which may be common (*blue, tall, pin-striped*) or proper (*French, American*); demonstrative ("*this* hot dog" as opposed to "*those* hot dogs"); and the articles *a, an,* and *the*. The definite article *the* is used to refer to a specific item or group of items ("*the* red teapots" as opposed to just any old teapots). The indefinite articles *a* and *an* are used when any item from a larger group might be indicated (in "*a* cat ran by," exactly *which* cat ran by is either unknown or unimportant). Use *an* instead of *a* when the following word begins with a vowel sound ("*an* eagle flew overhead").

Adverbs

While adjectives describe nouns, **adverbs** are modifiers that describe verbs, adjectives, and other adverbs. In "Julio laughs loudly," the adverb *loudly* describes the verb *laughs*. In "Her hair was very dark," the adverb *very* describes the adjective *dark*. In "The bus passed quite rapidly," the adverb *quite* describes another adverb, *rapidly*, which describes the verb *passed*.

Many adverbs have an -ly ending, especially those that are "built" from adjectives:

quick → quickly   happy → happily   double → doubly

Adverbs generally give information about when, where, why, how, how much, or how often something has occurred. For example, in "Sparky happily ran outside yesterday," *happily* tells how, *outside* tells where, and *yesterday* tells when.

Negatives and Double Negatives

Negatives are words such as *not, never, none, nothing, without*, and so on that can negate a statement, or change its meaning to the opposite of what it would mean without the negative. For example, "I never eat cookies" has an opposite meaning from "I eat cookies."

Be careful not to accidentally create a double negative by using two negative words where one will do. Depending on how they are used, they can essentially cancel each other out, changing the meaning of the statement to what it would mean without any negatives at all. For example, if you say "I did not eat no cookies," you are basically saying that you did eat some cookies—which is probably not what you really meant to say! The correct sentence would be something like "I did not eat any cookies."

Don't say I never warned you— watch out for double negatives!

Comparatives and Superlatives

The **comparative** form of an adjective or adverb shows that something has more or less of a particular quality compared to another item or items: "Jack is taller than Bill." The **superlative** form shows that something has the greatest or least amount of that quality compared to the other items in question: "Paul is the tallest boy on the team."

For most short adjectives or adverbs (one or two syllables long), add -er for the comparative or -est for the superlative. If the word already ends with -e, simply add -r or -st. If it ends with one vowel and one consonant, double the final consonant before adding -er or -est:

dark, darker, darkest   true, truer, truest   hot, hotter, hottest

For two-syllable words that end in -y, change the -y to -i before adding -er or -est:

happy, happier, happiest

For other words that have two or more syllables, use *more* or *most* to form the comparative or superlative:

gorgeous, more gorgeous, most gorgeous
interesting, more interesting, most interesting

Some adjectives and adverbs have irregular comparative and superlative forms. These include the adjectives *good* and *bad* and the adverbs *well* and *badly*. It is probably best to memorize these if you are not already familiar with them:

Adjectives: good, better, best   bad, worse, worst
In "I got a good grade on that test," the adjective *good* modifies the noun *grade*.

Adverbs: well, better, best   badly, worse, worst
In "I did well on that test," the adverb *well* modifies the verb *did*.

Wow, That's Really Intense!

Intensifiers include adverbs such as *very, really, quite, somewhat,* and so on. They express the relative intensity of whatever word they modify—the amount or degree to which that word applies. For example, a class that is only *somewhat* boring is not as boring as one that is *excessively* boring.

Careless writers use too many intensifiers, or use the same ones over and over again, to the point where they can lose their effect—or at least make whatever is being written, um, *very* boring. *Really* and *very* are commonly overused in this way. Some writers also make the mistake of using intensifiers when they don't actually make sense or add any meaning to the sentence. For example, it would not make any sense to say "That shrub is very dead"—except for comic effect. It is either dead, or it isn't! So if you use an intensifier, make sure it makes sense—and make sure you really mean it!

Prepositions

A **preposition** usually helps describe the relationship between a particular noun or pronoun and the rest of the sentence. Common prepositions include *about, above, across, at, behind, beneath, by, down, for, from, in, into, near, on, of, off, out, through, up, with, within,* and *without.* In "Beth walked around the garden," the preposition *around* tells where Beth walked in relationship to the garden—around it rather than into it, through it, behind it, or so on.

A preposition is usually part of a **prepositional phrase** that includes the preposition, a noun or pronoun that is considered the object of the preposition, and all related modifiers. In the prepositional phrase "around the garden," *around* is the preposition, *garden* is the object of the preposition, and *the* modifies garden.

More About Prepositions

Some grammar fans feel you should never end a sentence with a preposition. In other words, they believe a preposition should always come before its object as part of a prepositional phrase, not after it somewhere else in the sentence:

> **Avoid:** <u>Whom</u> should I write <u>to</u>?
> **Better:** <u>To whom</u> should I write?

"To end with a preposition, or not to. That is the question . . ."

Others feel it is acceptable to end with a preposition, especially in casual speech or when the result would otherwise seem very awkward or overly formal. It is also acceptable when the preposition is actually considered part of the verb, as in *give away*, *give in*, and *pick up*:

> **Correct:** I will not <u>give away</u> the secret.
> **Also correct:** I will not <u>give</u> the secret <u>away</u>.

Your best bet, especially in formal writing, is to err on the side of caution and avoid ending with a preposition unless that is the only way your sentence makes sense.

Conjunctions

Conjunctions are words that connect, or join together, parts of a sentence. **Coordinating conjunctions**, such as *and*, *or*, and *but*, can be used to join together items that have equal rank or importance within the sentence. (*Co-* means with or together with; *-ordinate* has to do with order—in this case, order of importance. Items that can be coordinated can be ordered together with each other. They have equal importance.)

If each of the ideas joined by a coordinating conjunction were stated independently, the basic meaning would still be the same as in the original sentence. For example, instead of "I like Siamese cats, and Steve likes tabbies," you could write "I like Siamese cats. Steve likes tabbies."

The coordinating conjunction *and* is used when all of the items should be considered together: "Steve likes cars, trucks, and motorcycles." *Or* describes a choice: "You may have a cookie or some ice cream." *But* shows contrast: "The game was long, but exciting."

Correlative conjunctions, such as *either / or*, *neither / nor*, and *not only / but also*, are another type of coordinating conjunction. They are used in pairs: "The hill was not only steep, but also slippery." Notice how the items joined by these conjunctions can also be presented independently: "The hill was steep. The hill was slippery." It might not sound as elegant, but the basic meaning from the original sentence has not really changed.

Subordinating conjunctions, such as *although*, *because*, *before*, *if*, *since*, *unless*, *until*, and *while*, introduce items of lesser rank or importance within the sentence. (*Sub-* means under or less than.) The ideas joined together by a subordinating conjunction cannot be stated independently without affecting the basic meaning of the original sentence. For example, in place of "The cat ran because the dog barked," you could not simply write "The cat ran. The dog barked." The relationship between the two ideas is no longer clear.

Why is the information introduced by a subordinating conjunction considered less important? Generally speaking, most subordinating conjunctions introduce information that helps explain things such as how, when, where, or why the main action of the sentence took place. Using our example above, the beginning of the original sentence could stand alone: "The cat ran." That is the main idea of the sentence, the main activity. The rest of the sentence, "because the dog barked," is considered interesting information but not essential to the main point. Here's one way to think about it: If the main action had never happened in the first place, there would be no reason to explain how, when, where, or why it happened!

Interjections

Interjections are "extra" words or phrases that are often used to express strong feelings, such as "Wow!" or "How true!" They may be complete sentences, as in "How pretty you are!" They might introduce a sentence, as in "Gosh, I never thought of that before." They might interrupt a thought: "As I was speaking—and a beautiful speech it was!—a fairly large tomato landed on the stage."

An interjection typically ends with an exclamation point to express excitement, although an interjection at the beginning of a sentence might end with a comma.

When you break a sentence down into different parts to see the purpose each part serves, this stuff can actually start to make more sense instead of less. It can also help you be a better writer—by knowing exactly what you are writing, and why!

Chapter Two

The Simple Sentence—and Beyond!

The last chapter covered the basic parts of speech. Now we'll take a look at how to combine them into different kinds of sentences—and how to avoid some common mistakes.

What Is a Sentence?

You might think of a sentence as just a group of words with a capital letter at the beginning and a period at the end, but there's actually a bit more to it than that. At the very least, a **complete sentence** must have one complete subject and one complete predicate that work together to communicate a complete thought. What's *that* mean, you ask? Keep reading . . .

The **complete subject** of a sentence includes a noun or pronoun—the **simple subject**—that tells who or what the sentence is about. It identifies the person or thing performing the main action of the sentence. The **complete predicate** includes a verb—the **simple predicate**—that tells what the subject does or is. It identifies the main action of the sentence. Although it is short, the following sentence is complete:

Nora runs.

It has a subject and a predicate and expresses a complete thought. At the end of the sentence, you know who does what. Although more information could be added, no information is obviously missing. Nothing else is required for this sentence to make sense.

In the sample sentence above, the simple subject "Nora" is also the complete subject. The simple predicate "runs" is also the complete predicate. As you can probably guess, though, sentences can get a bit more complicated than that! There are also many different kinds of sentences. Let's look a bit closer.

What Kind of Sentence Is It?

There are many different kinds of sentences, which serve different purposes. A **declarative sentence** is an ordinary statement that ends with a period. Most sentences are declarative: "The bus stops here." An **interrogative sentence** asks a question and ends with a question mark. Interrogative sentences are also inverted, or turned around—a verb comes before the subject: "Where is the bus?" An **exclamatory sentence** expresses strong feeling and ends with an exclamation point: "There it is!" An **imperative sentence**, or command, might end with either a period or an

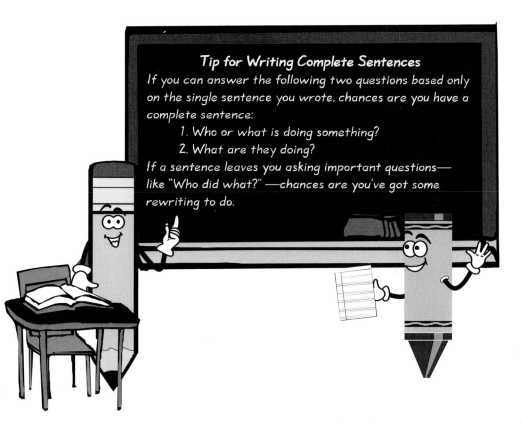

Tip for Writing Complete Sentences

If you can answer the following two questions based only on the single sentence you wrote, chances are you have a complete sentence:

1. Who or what is doing something?
2. What are they doing?

If a sentence leaves you asking important questions—like "Who did what?" —chances are you've got some rewriting to do.

exclamation point. Since the subject of an imperative sentence is understood to be "you," it may be left out: "Stop!"

The different kinds of sentences described in the last paragraph have to do with the general purpose the sentence serves. But there is another way of classifying sentences that has to do with how simple or complex the sentence is.

Simple Sentences

The **simple sentence** is the most basic kind of complete sentence, expressing a complete thought with only one complete subject and one complete predicate. But even that may be not so, uh, simple—so hang on to your hat!

A complete subject must include at least a simple subject (say, "Bob"), but might also include other words that identify the subject further ("Bob from the auto body shop"). Similarly, a complete predicate must include at least a simple predicate ("works," for example), but might also include other words that help describe the action further ("works like a dog all day"). Although one looks more complicated than the other, both of these complete sentences are simple sentences, since each has only one complete subject and one complete predicate:

> Bob works.
> Bob from the auto body shop works like a dog all day.

A simple sentence might actually have a compound subject, two or more individual subjects acting together: "Kashira and Jack ran for the door." Is that confusing? Since they act together, they are still considered part of one complete subject. A simple sentence might also have a compound predicate, two or more individual actions performed by the same subject: "Jack opened the door, ran toward the parking lot, and jumped into his car." Again, even though there are multiple actions, they are all being performed by the same subject, and are therefore considered part of one complete predicate. A simple sentence can even have both a compound subject and a compound predicate: "The driver and the passenger looked at each other and screamed."

A simple sentence that is an imperative, or command, might seem to include only a predicate and no subject: "Jump!" But in this case, remember, the subject is understood to be "you." You are being commanded to jump.

Here are some examples of simple sentences—sentences that have only one complete subject (no matter how complicated) and one complete predicate (no matter how complicated). In each example, a slash mark separates the complete subject from the complete predicate. The simple subjects are <u>underlined once</u>. The simple predicates are <u>underlined twice</u>:

> <u>Paul</u> / <u>cooks</u>.
> That tall <u>girl</u> with the curly hair / <u>is</u> taller than Nora.
> <u>Bill</u> and <u>Mario</u>, both good runners, / quickly <u>raced</u> home.
> <u>Hurry</u>! (The subject is understood to be "you.")

A sentence might include other nouns or pronouns in addition to the simple subject. It might have other verbs beyond the simple predicate. If you need to identify the simple subject or simple predicate, it can help to ask, "Who or what is performing or experiencing which main action or state of being?" Consider this example:

> Tomas ran to catch up with the dog.

This sentence has two nouns, "Tomas" and "dog," but which one is the simple subject? Two actions are described, "ran" and "catch up," but which one is the simple predicate? Tomas is performing the main action, "ran." Therefore "Tomas" is the simple subject and "ran" is the simple predicate. You could write "Tomas ran" and still have a complete sentence. The rest of the sentence adds more information but is not required to make the sentence complete.

Phrases and Clauses

Before we get into more complicated sentences, it will help to know about phrases and clauses. A **phrase** is a group of words that work together to express an idea.

A phrase may appear within a sentence, but does not form a complete sentence by itself. It lacks a subject, a predicate, or both:

the long and winding road   across the street
as quickly as possible   to buy milk

A **clause** is a group of words that work together to express an idea and include both a subject and a predicate. An **independent clause** has a subject and a predicate and expresses a complete thought. It could stand alone to form a complete simple sentence. A **dependent clause** has a subject and a predicate, but it does not communicate a complete thought. It cannot stand alone as a complete sentence; its meaning depends on the rest of the sentence. In other words, you need the rest of the sentence to help you figure out what's going on. In the following example, the dependent clause is underlined:

<u>While Kathleen went to the store</u>, I played video games.

"I played video games" is an independent clause. It has a subject (I) and a predicate (played video games) and can stand alone as a complete sentence. All by itself, it expresses a complete thought. "While Kathleen went to the store" is a dependent clause. It cannot stand alone as a complete sentence. It has a subject (Kathleen) and a predicate (went to the store), but it does not express a complete thought. Without the rest of the sentence, the reader is left wondering what happened while Kathleen went to the store. Dependent clauses begin with subordinating conjunctions such as *after, although, as, because, before, even if, even though, if, in order to, since, though, unless, until, whatever, when, whenever, whether, which,* and *while.*

Compound and Complex Sentences

In a **compound sentence**, two or more independent clauses are joined together by a comma and a coordinating conjunction (such as *and*, *or*, or *but*) or by a semicolon:

> Sofia ran fast, but Steve ran faster.
> The store was out of milk; they bought juice.

In a **complex sentence**, an independent clause is joined with at least one dependent clause. A dependent clause at the beginning of a sentence should be set off by a comma. (Once again, the dependent clauses in these examples are underlined.)

> They buy juice whenever the store is out of milk.
> Although it is getting dark, they walk home slowly.

Are you ready for this? A **compound-complex sentence** is essentially a compound sentence with at least two independent clauses. But it also includes at least one dependent clause:

> Sofia wore her parka because it was snowing, but Steve wore only a light jacket.

> When it is cold, Sofia always wears gloves; Steve is less careful.

Incomplete Sentences and Sentence Fragments

An **incomplete sentence** or **sentence fragment** is a word or group of words, such as a phrase or a dependent clause, that is written as if it were a complete sentence. These might be correct to use for dialogue, since people do often speak in incomplete sentences. For example, you might answer the question "What did you have for lunch?" with a single word, "Pizza." However, they are usually considered incorrect. Here are some more examples:

> The boy in the blue sweatshirt.
> *(What did the boy do? This incomplete sentence has a subject, but no predicate.)*

> Picked a whole bushel of strawberries.
> *(Who picked the strawberries? This incomplete sentence has a predicate, but no subject. This is different from a command, in which the subject is understood to be "you.")*

> At Mr. Pickalot's farm.
> *(Who did what at the farm? This incomplete sentence has no subject and no predicate.)*

> Whenever the car starts.
> *(What happens whenever the car starts? This incomplete sentence has a subject and a predicate, but it does not express a complete thought.)*

Uh-oh, the artist forgot to make me complete. I must be a cartoon fragment!

Run-on Sentences

Instead of not having enough information, a **run-on sentence** gives too much information. It includes two or more independent clauses that are not connected properly. Often, the independent clauses in a run-on sentence are joined only by a comma. This is also called a comma splice. A comma alone is not "strong enough" to join two independent clauses. Here is an example of a run-on sentence that features a comma splice:

> Rachel planted flowers, I sat in the sun and read.

Depending on your intended meaning, you can correct a run-on sentence in multiple ways. You can rewrite the independent clauses as separate sentences:

> Rachel planted flowers. I sat in the sun and read.

You can connect them with a semicolon or with a comma and a coordinating conjunction, forming a compound sentence:

> Rachel planted flowers; I sat in the sun and read.
> Rachel planted flowers, but I sat in the sun and read.

You can also make one of the clauses dependent by introducing it with a subordinating conjunction, forming a complex sentence. Remember to use a comma after a dependent clause at the beginning of a sentence:

> Rachel planted flowers while I sat in the sun and read.
> While Rachel planted flowers, I sat in the sun and read.

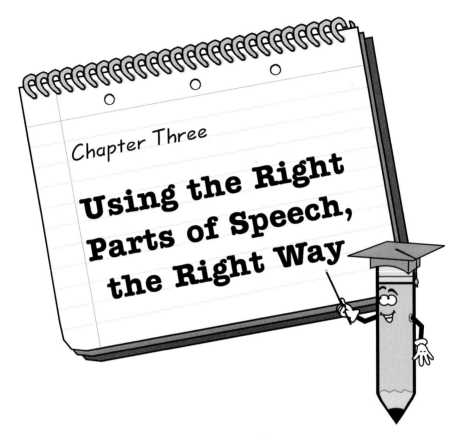

Chapter Three

Using the Right Parts of Speech, the Right Way

So far, we've covered the different parts of speech and different kinds of sentences—and some mistakes to avoid. Now we're going to look a little closer at how the different parts of speech work together within sentences.

You know that a sentence needs at least a subject (a noun or pronoun) and a predicate (a verb). But did you know that pronouns have to "agree" with the nouns they refer to, or that pronouns have different forms for different purposes? Did you know that a subject and verb also have to "agree," and that verbs have different forms depending on whether the action occurs in the past, present, or future? Let's see how all these things work together.

Subjects and Objects

You already know that a noun or pronoun can serve as a **subject**—a person, place, or thing that performs an action or experiences a state of being in a sentence. The proper noun "Mary" is the subject in this sentence:

Mary baked Sam a cake with frosting.

But nouns and pronouns can serve other purposes as well. For example, a **direct object** is a person, place, or thing to which the main action is done. In our sample sentence above, "cake" is a direct object—it is the thing that Mary baked. An **indirect object** is a person, place, or thing for which the main action is done to the direct object. "Sam" is the indirect object in our sample sentence—he is the person Mary baked the cake for. An **object of a preposition** is a person, place, or thing that is being described in relationship to some other part of the sentence. "Frosting" is the object of the preposition "with" in our sample sentence—it is the thing the cake came with.

What Kind of Subject Is It?

One important thing to know about the subject of a sentence is its **number**. In other words, is it singular (one person, place, or thing) or plural (more than one person, place, or thing)? Its **gender** is also important—a subject is considered neuter if it names something that has no gender (such as a paperclip), indefinite if it has a gender that is unknown (such as a stray dog), masculine if it is known to be male, and feminine if it is known to be female. Another important quality of the subject has to do with **person**. You may be familiar with the terms first person, second person, and third person. Let's take a look at what they're all about.

When the subject of the sentence speaks or writes about himself or herself (or themselves), that is considered first person. Another way to think about that is to imagine there is only one person (or group of people) involved: the person (or group of people) speaking or writing. "I" is a first person, singular subject. "We" is a first person, plural subject. "Tom and I," "my friends and I," and "those of us who like to surf" are other possible examples of first person, plural subjects; each of them could be replaced by "we" and basically mean the same thing.

When the speaker or writer of the sentence is speaking or writing directly to another person (or group of people), that is considered second person. Here, imagine there are two people (or groups of people) involved: whoever is speaking, and whomever they are speaking to. "You" is a second person subject, which may be either singular or plural.

Third person is used when the speaker or writer of the sentence is speaking or writing about another person, place, or thing (or group of people, places, or things). In this case, you can think of three people (or groups) being involved: whoever is speaking, whomever they are speaking to, and whomever or whatever they are speaking about. "He," "she," "it," "Pablo," "the dog," and "New York City" are all possible examples of third person, singular subjects. "They," "Stefan, Lisa, and Caitlin," "cats," and "all the cities I've ever been to" are all possible examples of third person, plural subjects.

Pronoun-Antecedent Agreement

Number, gender, and person are important for **pronoun-antecedent agreement**, or making sure any pronouns you use match up with their antecedents (the nouns they replace or refer to). For example, a third person, plural pronoun should be used for a third person, plural noun.

The <u>dogs</u> barked all night. <u>They</u> must be tired!

Gender comes into play for third person, singular pronouns. If the antedecent is third person, singular, and clearly refers to a female, any pronouns that refer to it should be third person, singular, and feminine (*she, her, hers,* or *herself*). If the antecedent is third person, singular, and clearly refers to a male, any pronouns that refer to it should be third person, singular, and masculine (*he, him, his,* or *himself*). Otherwise, use the indefinite or neuter third person, singular pronouns (*it, its,* or *itself*), which do not indicate gender:

<u>Sheila</u> brought <u>her</u> best friend to the party.
<u>Carl</u> is a loner. <u>He</u> likes to sit all by <u>himself</u>.
The <u>dog</u> ran to <u>its</u> water bowl.

Pronoun Cases

Pronouns have different forms depending on their case, or the purpose they serve in the sentence. You probably already use most of them correctly without even thinking about it.

The subjective case includes pronouns such as *I, you, she, he, it, we, they, who,* and *whoever.* You will use the subjective case when the pronoun is being used as a subject in the sentence, as in "I left school early to go to a dentist appointment." The subject of this sentence is "I."

The objective case includes pronouns such as *me, you, her, him, it, us, them, whom,* and *whomever.* The objective case is used when the pronoun is serving as a direct or indirect object of a verb or as the object of a preposition:

> **Direct object:** The teacher punished <u>them</u>.
> **Indirect object:** Mohammed brought <u>her</u> some lunch.
> **Object of a preposition:** The girls ran away from <u>us</u>.

Reflexive pronouns are used when an object refers back to, or reflects, the subject of the sentence. The reflexive pronouns end in -self (for singular) or -selves (for plural) and include *myself, yourself, herself, himself, itself, ourselves, yourselves,* and *themselves*:

> <u>I</u> made <u>myself</u> a nice lunch.
> The <u>dancers</u> were proud of <u>themselves</u>.

The possessive case includes the pronouns *my, your, his, her, its, our, their,* and *whose*. These stand in place

Reflecting on Reflexives

The reflexive form of a pronoun may sometimes be used as an intensive pronoun, adding extra emphasis to another noun or pronoun in the sentence. For example, instead of saying "He opened the jar," you might say "He opened the jar himself." This calls special attention to the fact that he actually did it himself as opposed to, say, needing his little sister's help. Try to use an intensive pronoun only when there really is a need for such special emphasis. Otherwise, it is just repetitive information.

While we're on the subject of reflexives, be sure to use the plural ending (-selves) when you're referring to more than one person, place, or thing, not the singular ending (-self):

> **Incorrect:** They gave themself a raise.
> **Correct:** They gave themselves a raise.

Also be sure to use the correct form of the pronoun before adding -self or -selves. Common errors include using *hisself* instead of *himself,* or *theirselves* instead of *themselves*.

of a possessive noun. For example, "That is Paula's shoe!" becomes "That is her shoe!"

Absolute possessive pronouns include *mine, yours, his, hers, its, ours,* and *theirs.* These stand in place of both the possessive noun and the thing that is owned: "That is Paula's shoe!" becomes "That is hers!" Absolute possessives should only be used when it would be very clear to the listener or reader exactly what is owned.

Guide to Pronoun Case and Person			
Person, Number, Gender	**Subjective Case**	**Objective Case / Reflexive Form**	**Possessive Case / Absolute Form**
1st Person, Singular	I	me / myself	my / mine
2nd Person, Singular	you	you / yourself	your / yours
3rd Person, Singular Feminine Masculine Indefinite or Neuter	 she he it	 her / herself him / himself it / itself	 her / hers his / his its / its
1st Person, Plural	we	us / ourselves	our / ours
2nd Person, Plural	you	you / yourself	your / yours
3rd Person, Plural	they	them / themselves	their / theirs

Subject-Verb Agreement

You read earlier about pronoun-antecedent agreement, making sure a pronoun matches the noun it replaces or refers to in terms of number (singular or plural), gender (masculine, feminine, indefinite, or neuter), and person (first, second, or third). A similar process is involved in **subject-verb agreement**, or making sure the verb form you use matches the subject in number and person. That sounds kind of daunting, but the good news is that most verbs don't change all that much. In fact, the only time you really have to worry about this is with the present tense, the verb form used for events happening at the present moment, or "now." Since this goes hand in hand with learning the present tense, it will be covered in that section below.

Verb Tenses

Did you know that verbs can tell time? Well, not really—but verbs do have different tenses. The **tense** helps show when an event occurs, such as in the past, in the present, or in the future. There are several verb tenses to learn, so let's dig in!

Present Tense

The present tense is used to describe actions that happen in the present—things that are happening "now" at the current time:

> They sail across the river.

The present tense might also be used to describe events in the past or future, if that time frame has already been clearly established and it would be awkward or boring to keep using the past or future tense. The present tense also includes actions that happen regularly in the present ("this clock strikes every hour") and things that are generally true all the time ("mountains are tall").

The tricky part of the present tense has to do with subject-verb agreement, making sure the verb matches the subject in terms of number (singular or plural) and person (first, second, or third). Regular verbs in the present tense only have one change to think about— adding an -s when the subject is third person, singular:

	Singular	Plural
1st Person	I cook	we cook
2nd Person	you cook	you cook
3rd Person	he / she / it cooks	they cook

Just as with certain plural nouns, verbs that end with -ch, -sh, -s, -x, or -z may add -es rather than simply adding -s. Verbs that end with a consonant plus -y may change the -y to -i and add -es.

I / we / you / they pass   he / she / it passes
I / we / you / they fly   he / she / it flies

The problems really start with irregular verbs. They follow a different pattern than regular verbs—their spelling changes in different ways. These can get a little complicated. Some of the most common are the verbs *be* and *have*:

I am	we are	I have	you have
you are	you are	you have	we have
he / she / it is	they are	he / she / it has	they have

You may already know or have memorized many irregular verbs. If not, the chart on page 58 lists several. Your dictionary can also be helpful for both regular and

Reaching an Agreement Can Be Tricky!

Subject-verb and pronoun-antecedent agreement can pose some interesting problems. For example, a list of two or more nouns or pronouns joined by *and* is generally treated as a plural. But if the items are joined by *or*, the form of any verbs or pronouns that refer to the list is generally determined by the last item on the list:

> Both the library and the bank close their doors at 5:00.
> Either the library or the bank closes its doors at 5:00.
> Either the library or the banks close their doors at 5:00.

Collective nouns such as *audience*, *team*, and *group* describe multiple items as part of a group—one collective whole that includes several individual members. This can pose a problem when figuring out subject-verb or pronoun-antecedent agreement. If the group represented by the collective noun is acting as a single unit, it should be treated as a singular noun. If the members of the group are obviously acting as separate individuals, related verbs and pronouns should be plural:

> If the team wins this game, it will be in the playoffs.
> The audience clapped their hands.

Indefinite pronouns can also be a little tricky. Although they may have a plural sense in some cases, pronouns such as *anything*, *everyone*, and *none* are generally considered singular:

> **Incorrect:** Everyone think their own child is perfect.
> **Correct:** Everyone thinks his or her own child is perfect.

While we're on that subject, though, some people feel it is acceptable to use "their" in place of a phrase like "his or her" if that phrase would seem too awkward, or as an alternative to using only "his" or only "her" (which might seem biased in favor of one gender or the other). If you are writing for someone else, such as a teacher, it can help to find out ahead of time which approach they prefer.

irregular verbs. If you know a main verb, such as "carry," you can look that up. If there are any special spellings you need to know, they should also be shown as part of that main entry. If you know a special verb form, such as "is," you should also be able to look that up as a main entry. Your dictionary should tell you what main verb it is a form of and exactly which form it is—in other words, when it should be used. For example, your dictionary should show that "is" is the third person, singular, present tense form of the verb "be."

Your dictionary might also have a special section or chart that shows common verb forms. At the very least, the front or back of your dictionary should include an explanation of how the different verb forms are shown in that particular dictionary.

Past Tense

The past tense is used when you are writing about things that have already happened:

> They sailed across the river yesterday.

The past tense of regular verbs is formed by adding -ed:

cook → cooked	open → opened
watch → watched	play → played

As with other spelling rules you've learned, there are some exceptions. For example, for most verbs that end with -e, just add -d; for most that end with a consonant and -y, change the -y to -i and add -ed:

believe → believed	race → raced
cry → cried	try → tried

For most verbs that end with a vowel plus a consonant and have only one syllable—or more than one syllable but with the stress on the final syllable—double the final consonant and add -ed:

crop → cropped   skip → skipped

refer → referred   occur → occurred

But again, some verbs do not follow a simple formula. Here are some common verbs with irregular past tense forms:

be → was   have → had

go → went   fly → flew

ring → rang   bring → brought

buy → bought   catch → caught

Are you seeing a pattern there? Neither am I! Actually, there *are* some patterns you can learn for certain kinds of irregular verbs. The problem is that the list of irregular verbs is rather long, and the patterns are, well, kind of strange. You may form a lot of them correctly without even thinking about it, or you may be able to memorize several of them. But if not, once again a good dictionary can be extremely helpful. The entry for the main verb should include any irregular forms, and you should also be able to look up any irregular forms as separate entries to find out what verb and tense they are for. Also see the chart on page 58.

Future Tense

Verbs in the future tense use "will" before the main form of the verb to indicate that the action will happen in the future, at some point after the current moment:

They will sail across the river tomorrow.

Progressive Tense

The past, present, and future progressive tenses describe actions that are ongoing—"in progress"—at the

Helping Verbs and Split Infinitives

Verbs such as *be, can, do, have, may,* and *will* can serve as auxiliary or helping verbs. A helping verb comes before the main verb it is working with and changes to agree with the subject and reflect the correct tense. The main verb may be separated, or split, from the helping verb by other modifying words. The subject of the sentence may also come between the helping verb and the main verb to form a question.

> Today, I can go to the mall. Yesterday, I could not go.
> Did you see that huge wave? No, but I do see a shark fin!

This brings up another grammar issue, the split infinitive. The infinitive is a special verb form that combines the preposition *to* with the main form of a verb: *to go, to run, to play,* and so on. Many people believe you should avoid splitting an infinitive whenever possible. For example, if you are using the infinitive *to have,* then no other words should come between *to* and *have.* Others feel it is acceptable—or even in some cases more correct—to do so. This is especially true when the word that splits the infinitive is being given special emphasis.

> **Awkward:** I prefer to quickly walk.
> **Better:** I prefer to walk quickly.
> **Also correct:** I have learned to always check my work.

point of time in question. They are formed by using either the past, present, or future tense of "be" (underlined once in the examples on the next page) along with the present participle of the main verb (underlined twice on the next page).

The present participle of most verbs is formed by adding -ing. For most verbs that end with a consonant and -e, remove the -e before adding -ing (chase → chasing). For most one- or two-syllable verbs that end with one vowel and one consonant, double the final consonant before adding -ing (occur → occurring).

Past progressive:	While Dale <u>was eating</u>, his mother shopped.
Present progressive:	I <u>am cooking</u> now.
Future progressive:	He <u>will be speaking</u> to the students once a month.

Perfect Tense

Most people think of "perfect" as meaning "without any flaws," but another sense of it means "complete." The past, present, and future perfect tenses describe actions

The Case of the Misplaced Modifier

When you can't tell which part of a sentence is being modified by a particular word or phrase, or if the part that appears to be modified makes no sense, you are probably dealing with a misplaced modifier. Look at this example:

While running, the branch scraped Evan's arm.

So, how fast was the branch running? The phrase "while running" appears to modify the subject "branch," but most likely Evan was doing the running. This kind of error can lead to some pretty amusing results—or even some serious consequences! Here are some corrected versions:

The branch scraped Evan's arm while he was running.
While running, Evan scraped his arm on the branch.
Evan scraped his arm on the branch while running.

The last two suggestions point to another problem in our original sentence, which is also present in the first corrected version above. Those sentences might leave the reader with the impression that the branch acted on its own to scratch Evan's arm, whether on purpose or by accident. And unless this is some kind of weird dream or fantasy story, that isn't very likely. All in all, this just further proves that you must be very careful to make sure your sentences say exactly what you mean them to say!

Verb Tense Consistency

Once you establish that the action in a sentence, paragraph, or longer piece of writing occurs at a certain point in time, you should generally stick to that same time frame throughout. Usually, that means using the same verb tense. In other words, if you start off in the past tense, don't just switch randomly to the present or future tense. It may be appropriate to switch tenses, though, if you are clearly referring to things that happen at different times.

Incorrect: Yesterday I walked to the store. I stop by Cammie's house on the way.

Correct: Yesterday I walked to the store. I stopped by Cammie's house on the way.

Also correct: Yesterday I walked to the store. I had visited with Cammie earlier that day, so I did not stop by her house. Tomorrow, I will see Cammie again.

Here's another thing. Most people feel it is better to use the active voice than the passive voice. Huh? In the active voice, the subject of the sentence is clearly performing the action. In the passive voice, the subject is acted upon. You may need to use the passive voice sometimes. For example, you may not know—or it may not really matter—who actually performed the action. But whenever possible, try to use the active voice:

Passive: The cake was stolen.

Active: The thief stole the cake.

that are already complete, or "perfect," at the point of time in question. They are formed by using the past, present, or future tense of "have" (underlined once on the next page) plus the past participle of the main verb (underlined twice on the next page).

The past participle of most verbs is formed by adding -ed. For most verbs that end with a consonant and -e, remove the -e before adding -ed (chase → chased). For most one- or two-syllable verbs that end with one vowel and one consonant, double the final consonant before adding -ed (occur → occurred). However, just like with the past tense, many verbs have irregular forms for the past participle (be → been, have → had, go → gone, ring → rung, and so on). Again, the chart on page 58 or a good dictionary can help with these.

Past perfect: The winning team had gone by the time the crowd rushed out of the stands an hour ago.

Present perfect: As of today, Anna has traveled to every state in the country.

Future perfect: We will have succeeded by the time the teacher returns tomorrow.

Perfect Progressive Tense

This may start to seem very confusing, but hang in there! This is a combination of the last few ideas. The past, present, and future perfect progressive tenses describe actions that were once ongoing or continuing ("in progress") but are already complete ("perfect") at the point of time in question. They use the past, present, or future perfect tense of "be" (*had been, has been* or *have been, will have been*; underlined once below) along with the present participle of the main verb, which helps show that an action is ongoing or continuing (the -ing form of the main verb; underlined twice below).

Past perfect progressive: My mom had been knitting a sweater when she ran out of wool yesterday.

Present perfect progressive: As of today, they have been searching for the lost keys for three weeks.

Future perfect progressive: By next month, I will have been writing in my journal for six years.

Chapter Four

Punctuation, Proofreading, and Other Fine Points

Now that you are familiar with parts of speech and the grammatical structures of sentences, it is time to talk about some other elements that go into picture-perfect writing.

Punctuation

Proper punctuation helps people read and understand your writing. It helps clarify what you mean and how your ideas fit together.

Period

A period (.) should be used at the end of every sentence, unless the sentence requires a question mark or exclamation mark instead. Declarative sentences—regular statements that are neither direct questions nor exclamations—end with a period. Indirect questions and

All aboard at the Punctuation Station!

some imperative sentences, or commands, also end with periods.

> My garden is overrun with grubs and beetles.
> He asked when it would rain.
> Go to the store.

Periods are also used with some abbreviations. You will learn more about abbreviations later in this chapter.

Question Mark

A question mark (?) should be used at the end of an interrogative sentence, a sentence that asks a direct question. A verb comes before the subject in an interrogative sentence. A question might also begin with *who, what, where, why, when,* or *how.*

> Did you run all the way to school?
> How is Fred?

Exclamation Point

An exclamation point (!) is used at the end of an exclamatory sentence to express excitement, surprise, horror, or some other strong emotion. A command might also end with an exclamation point. An exclamation point is also often used after an interjection, a word or phrase used to express strong emotion.

> I can't believe she said that during class!
> Go to the store now!
> Wow! Taniqua is a great singer.

Comma

A comma (,) is used to separate different parts of a sentence. Commas are used in the following situations:

- To join two independent clauses with a coordinating conjunction.
  > I lost my wallet, but Jim lent me some money.

- After an introductory or transition word or phrase at the beginning of a sentence.
  > Some people like to pull dogs' tails. However, most dogs do not like people to pull their tails.

- After a dependent clause at the beginning of a sentence.
  > Because she did not want to get any more tardy slips, Melissa began waking up ten minutes earlier each day.

- To set off a nonessential part of a sentence.
  > The circus, which was in town for only one day, attracted a huge crowd.

- To set off a quote from the rest of the sentence.
  > "I won't forget my jacket," Lee told his mother, "because I left it right by the door."

- Between two or more adjectives or adverbs that modify the same word. If you could use "and" between them and mean the same thing, you can use a comma instead.

  The tired, relieved duck swam away from the dark brown dog.

  There is a comma between "tired" and "relieved" because they both modify the same word, "duck." There is no comma between "dark" and "brown" because "dark" modifies "brown."

- To set off the parts of a date or address.

  The movie will be showing from December 21, 2005, to January 18, 2006.

  Susan lives in Columbus, Ohio.

  Sean lived in Dublin, Ireland, before moving to the United States.

- To separate items in a list. Some people prefer to include a terminal comma, a comma before the last item in the list.

  He met John, Mary and Sam at the party.

  He met John, Mary, and Sam at the party.

I think I'll put commas everywhere, just to be on the safe side.

Colon

A colon (:) can be used to introduce a word, a phrase, or a list. A colon might also be used to introduce an independent clause. Using a colon can help add emphasis to whatever follows. Try not to overuse them. The next page includes some examples of how to use colons correctly.

By noon I had just one thing on my mind: lunch.

Of all my friends, only three like to swim: Nora, Natalie, and Jack.

There is a solution to this problem: You can do things my way!

If you use a colon to introduce a list, make sure it is actually a list and not just the rest of your sentence. If a colon appears immediately after a verb or the word *to*, it may be a hint that the colon is being used incorrectly.

Incorrect: I like: fish, spinach, and peanut butter.
Correct: I like fish, spinach, and peanut butter.

Incorrect: The teacher asked me to: write a paper, finish my math homework, and give an oral report.
Correct: The teacher asked me to do a lot of work: write a paper, finish my math homework, and give an oral report.

Semicolon

A semicolon (;) can be used to connect two independent clauses in a compound sentence. It is also used to separate parts of a complex list, a list containing items or groups of items that already have commas.

I went to the concert last night; the band was on fire!

The choices for breakfast this morning are cereal and fruit; eggs, bacon and toast; or pancakes, sausage, and home fries.

Apostrophe

An apostrophe (') takes the place of the missing letter or letters in a contraction, as shown in the examples on the next page.

I am → I'm	is not → isn't
you are → you're	cannot → can't
we are → we're	do not → don't

While contractions are often used in speech, they are not usually appropriate to use in formal writing.

An apostrophe plus -s is used for the possessive form of most nouns. Use an apostrophe alone for the possessive form of plural nouns that end with -s.

Singular:
Henry's car   James's gift   the horse's mouth

Plural that does not end with -s:
the men's coats   the people's rights

Plural that ends with -s:
the cats' tails   the Smiths' driveway

Quotation Marks

Quotation marks (" ") are used for direct quotes. They show that somebody is speaking or that you are quoting someone word for word. They can also be used to set off a special word or the title of a book or other such work. It is important to know how to capitalize and punctuate quotations—they can be confusing!

To introduce most full quotes in the middle of a sentence, use a comma before the opening quotation mark. The quote should also begin with a capital letter. Periods, question marks, exclamation points, and commas at the end of such quotes go inside the closing quotation mark. Colons and semicolons go outside the closing quotation mark.

"Why are you leaving now?" asked Suzanne.
Jorge said, "My class starts in five minutes," then left.

> Beverly added, "I can't believe it's already time to go."
>
> Bill said, "Run to the store"; he knew it was closing.

If only part of what you are quoting is a direct, word-for-word quote, you may not need to start with a capital or set it off with commas. This is also true if you are using the quotation marks to set off a special word or a title. If this kind of quote comes at the end of a sentence, the closing period still usually goes inside the quotation marks. For question marks and exclamation points, however, it would depend on whether it is part of the actual quote or part of the longer sentence.

> She described the sunrise as "a peach parfait."
>
> How do you pronounce "parfait"?
>
> For the audition, she sang "Oklahoma!"

Use single quotation marks if what you are quoting appears within another direct quote.

> Paul said, "Right in the middle of the movie, someone shouted 'Fire!'"

Indirect quotes do not require quotation marks.

> Mr. Ethan said he had never heard such bad singing.

Hyphen

A hyphen (-) is used for some compound words, which you will learn about later in this chapter. Hyphens are also used to spell out numbers between twenty-one and ninety-nine. You may also see hyphens in books and other printed works to show that a word is continuing to the next line; such breaks should occur between syllables, not just anywhere in the word.

Certain prefixes require the use of hyphens (as in

ex-boyfriend, self-serve, and *all-consuming).* You should also use a hyphen if the prefix comes before a word that must be capitalized, or if the prefix itself must be capitalized (*non-English, A-frame).* You may need to use a hyphen if the prefix ends with the same letter that the main word begins with (*re-enter, de-emphasize);* however, there are exceptions to this rule (*unnatural, cooperate).* When in doubt about hyphens, check your dictionary.

Some Special Cases

Compound Words

Sometimes two or more words are connected to make a new word with a distinct meaning. The result is called a compound word. There are three kinds of compound words: closed (*notebook, softball);* hyphenated (*six-pack, daughter-in-law);* and open (*post office, full moon).*

You might use a hyphen to create a temporary compound word if the meaning of a word or phrase could be confusing without it. Consider the phrase, "old coin collector." In this phrase, a reader can't tell if the coins are old or if the collector is old. Writing "old-coin collector" makes it a lot easier to understand that it is the coins that are old. To solve the same problem, you could also write "a collector of old coins."

Abbreviations and Acronyms

An abbreviation is a shortened form of a word or phrase. In many cases, it is not considered acceptable to use abbreviations in writing. However, some are quite common and are acceptable to use in writing without explanation. This is especially true for people's names and titles, as shown on the next page.

Dr. Rita Swanson

Mr. Sanghee

Thomas Montfair, Ph.D.

Abbreviations might also be used in writing when a longer name or phrase is going to be used frequently. In these cases, you should spell out the entire word or words the first time they are used. Then put the abbreviation in parentheses after the full name. That way the reader will know what the abbreviation stands for the next time it is used.

> Harry attended New York University (NYU) for his undergraduate degree. He was a strong candidate for the NYU journalism program.

Common measurements are also sometimes abbreviated, such as miles per hour (mph), feet (ft), or cubic centimeters (cc).

For the most part, use capital letters for abbreviations of proper nouns and lowercase letters for other abbreviations. Some abbreviations use periods, including titles such as "Mrs." or "Dr." before a person's name, but many do not require them. Fortunately—or unfortunately!—there are few strict rules about this. If you are not sure, check your dictionary. When an abbreviation that uses a period appears at the end of a sentence, you do not need to add another period.

An acronym is a type of abbreviation in which a new word is formed from the initial letters of a group of words. For example, NASA is an acronym for National Aeronautics and Space Administration. But instead of reading off each individual letter, "*n, a, s, a*," readers pronounce it as one word, "*nasa*." Some other acronyms include AIDS (acquired immunodeficiency syndrome) and NATO (North Atlantic Treaty Organization). Most acronyms are capitalized and use no periods.

Proofreading

Proofreading, or reading through something in order to find and correct mistakes, is the final step in making the grammar in your writing flawless. All great writers proofread their work. If you want to be a great writer too, it's time to proofread.

The best way to proofread your writing is to reread slowly. You can read it through several times, checking for different kinds of mistakes each time. Take each sentence individually and make sure you are using the right words, that each word is spelled correctly, and that all capitalization and punctuation are correct. Check to make sure each sentence is complete by pretending that none of the other sentences exist. Would it make sense on its own? If you find any run-on sentences, can they be fixed with conjunctions and proper punctuation, or should they be rewritten as two or more sentences?

Spell-Check Your Spell-Checker!

"I don't really need to check my spelling myself," you say, "because my computer has a spell-checker." Well, that's great. Spell-check is a very helpful feature if you use a word processing program to write. But in case you haven't already heard, spell-check is not always accurate! For example, you might misspell a word by typing another word that exists but is not the correct spelling for the word you want to use. You might intend to write, "Litter is a major part of the pollution problem in the United States." If you type it in with errors, you might end up with "**Liter** is a major **par off** the pollution problem **if** the **Unite** States." Your mistakes

Hmm . . . spotless spelling, super sentences, perfect punctuation, and great grammar. Proofreading complete!

Wow! That's great!

proofing checklist done

are actually real words, and spell-check will not know to correct them. It might actually flag some if you're also using a grammar-check, since this mistake-ridden sentence makes no sense—but even that is no guarantee. As you may have noticed, grammar is even trickier than spelling, and the computer might interpret things differently than you intended them.

Spell-check might also say that a word is misspelled even if it is not. Proper names are often flagged as misspelled in spell-check even if they are correct. Try typing your first and last name into a computer. Does spell-check recognize your name?

So, what should you do? Run spell-check, but also read your work through on your own. Have a good dictionary by your side. Consider each word individually, looking for any mistake. Use your dictionary to look up any word you are not completely sure of—and even some you think you are sure of. Longer words should be looked up, as well as any that you do not use regularly. It is better to look up too many than not enough!

After you have proofread your writing once, take a break for a while—maybe even overnight. Go back to your writing and proofread it again to make sure all the mistakes are really gone, and that you haven't made any new errors. If you suspect there is a mistake but you are not sure, ask a classmate, friend, or parent to take a look, and talk it out together.

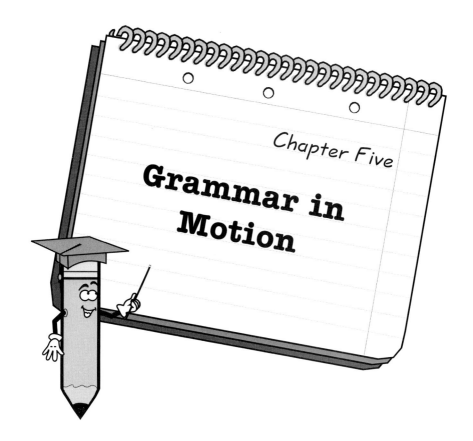

Chapter Five

Grammar in Motion

Part of the fun of grammar is that the rules are always changing. "WHAT?!" you say. "Does that mean I just learned all this stuff for nothing?" Not at all! But new words are always being formed, and new rules often come along with them. One of the best examples of this is from the world of computers. Look at all the words we have now that did not exist before: *e-mail, download, modem,* and *Internet* are just a few examples. Also, the way words are used can change, and once-strict rules may change as different patterns become accepted over time.

Remember too that even the best writers need to be reminded of the rules every once in a while. No one book can teach you all of the rules of grammar, but you are off to a great start. When you have questions, a good dictionary can be very helpful. You can use it to check spelling, to find out what part of speech a word is, to learn other words that mean the same thing, and more. A good dictionary is every great writer's best tool. After that, you can look up grammar questions in guidebooks like this one or on the Internet, or ask a teacher or someone else who is good at grammar and writing.

Grammar is designed to make your life easier. So keep your eyes open to ways that grammar can make reading and writing easier, and even more fun!

Grammar Is Cool!

We did it! Let's celebrate!

Common Grammar Goofs

Everyone makes grammar goofs sometimes. Certain kinds of mistakes are fairly common. Let's take a look at some.

Commonly Confused Words

The sample sentences below may help you remember some of the differences between these words people often confuse. If you'd like to learn more about them, check them out in your dictionary!

accept / except: I can *accept* your idea, *except* for the part about eating snails.

advise / advice: I *advise* you not to offer *advice* unless you are asked for it!

affect / effect: The actor wanted his speech to *affect* the audience, but I don't think it had the *effect* he hoped for.

already / all ready: Sam was *already* packed yesterday, so he is *all ready* to go.

altogether / all together: I am *altogether* shocked; *all together*, Tyrone ate sixteen donuts.

amount / number: This recipe involves a large *amount* of butter as well as a large *number* of chocolate chunks.

between / among: *Between* you and me, this information should stay *among* our group of friends.

can / may: "Mom, I *can* see Steve playing outside in his yard. *May* I go play with him?"

capital / capitol: The *Capitol* building is in the nation's *capital*, Washington, D.C., and is spelled with a *capital* letter.

compliment / complement: She paid me a *compliment*, saying the pie was a perfect *complement* to the meal.

desert / dessert: Please don't *desert* me in the *desert*; I don't want to be alone in this hot, sandy place. Also, I want to be home in time for some delicious chocolate *dessert*!

everyday / every day: Steve wore his *everyday* clothes to the park *every day* last week.

farther / further: I think that tree may be *farther* away than it seems; please investigate *further* by measuring the exact distance.

it's / its: As long as *it's* daylight, our dog can find *its* way home.

lay / lie: Today I *lay* the papers on the floor; yesterday I *laid* them on the table. Today I *lie* down at 9:00; yesterday I *lay* down at 9:30. Today I will not *lie* to my mother; yesterday I *lied* about where I went after school.

less / fewer: There would be *less* traffic in the morning if *fewer* people drove to work.

lessen / lesson: My embarrassing performance didn't *lessen* my desire for another piano *lesson*.

or / nor: I don't want ice cream *or* cake. Maria wants *neither* cookies *nor* cake.

principal / principle: The school *principal* told us never to forget the *principle* of helping others before helping yourself.

set / sit: *Set* your books on the table before you *sit* down.

stationary / stationery: Since the train was *stationary* due to a signal delay, I took out my *stationery* and wrote a letter.

than / then: First we walked for more *than* an hour, and *then* we rested.

their / there / they're: The girls said *their* books are over *there*, but *they're* going to read them over here.

who / whom: I know *who* asked for cake, but to *whom* should I give this piece of candy?

who's / whose: *Who's* going to tell me *whose* socks these are?

your / you're: *Your* shoes are too big, and *you're* stepping on my toes!

Commonly Misused Words

There are certain words that people often misuse. When others see or hear them used the wrong way, they may begin to think that way is correct. Here are a few; can you think of any others?

- "**A lot**" is correct; "alot" is not a word.
- Most grammar fans prefer "**all right**" to "alright."
- Say "**different from**," not "different than."
- "**Doubtless**" is correct, not "doubtlessly."
- Use "**regardless**." Avoid using "irregardless."
- "I **used to** like eggs" is correct; "use to" is incorrect.

Commonly Misspelled Words

Here are some words that are often misspelled. Although it helps to always have a dictionary nearby, it can also help to memorize some of these so you don't have to worry about them.

absence	discipline	lightning	quizzes
accidentally	eighth	maintenance	receive
arithmetic	embarrass	maneuver	recommend
athletic	exaggerate	marriage	rhyme
attendance	familiar	miniature	rhythm
belief	February	mysterious	schedule
business	foreign	ninety	separate
calendar	forty	noticeable	sergeant
changeable	fourth	occurred	sophomore
conscience	government	opinion	tragedy
conscientious	grammar	opportunity	undoubtedly
conscious	heroes	optimistic	unnecessary
criticize	independence	paid	until
deferred	intelligence	parallel	usually
desperate	knowledge	performance	weird
dictionary	laboratory	prejudice	yield

Some Common Irregular Verbs

Many grammar goofs have to do with irregular verbs. This chart may help you avoid making some of those mistakes.

Main Verb	3rd Person Present Tense	3rd Person Past Tense (Singular, Plural)	Past Participle
arise	arises	arose	arisen
be	is	was, were	been
begin	begins	began	begun
break	breaks	broke	broken
bring	brings	brought	brought
buy	buys	bought	bought
catch	catches	caught	caught
chose	chooses	chose	chosen
come	comes	came	come
do	does	did	done
drink	drinks	drank	drunk
drive	drives	drove	driven
eat	eats	ate	eaten
fight	fights	fought	fought
fly	flies	flew	flown
give	gives	gave	given
go	goes	went	gone
grow	grows	grew	grown
have	has	had	had
hide	hides	hid	hidden
know	knows	knew	known
lay	lays	laid	laid
lead	leads	led	led
lie	lies	lay	lain
light	lights	lit	lit
lose	loses	lost	lost
ride	rides	rode	ridden
ring	rings	rang	rung
run	runs	ran	run
see	sees	saw	seen
sing	sings	sang	sung
sit	sits	sat	sat
speak	speaks	spoke	spoken
swim	swims	swam	swum
take	takes	took	taken
tear	tears	tore	torn
write	writes	wrote	written

Glossary

adjective—A modifier that describes a noun or pronoun.

adverb—A modifier that describes a verb, adjective, or other adverb.

antecedent—The noun that a pronoun refers to. The antedecent should come before the pronoun.

clause—A group of words that work together and include both a subject and a predicate.

comparative—The form of an adjective or adverb that shows that something has more or less of a particular quality compared to another item or items.

complete predicate—The part of a sentence that includes the simple predicate, the verb identifying the main action or state of being in the sentence. The complete predicate may also include additional information or description beyond the simple predicate.

complete sentence—A group of words with at least one complete subject and predicate that work together to communicate a complete thought.

complete subject—The part of a sentence that includes the simple subject, a noun or pronoun identifying the person, place, or thing that performs the action or experiences the state of being in the sentence. The complete subject may also include additional identifying information or description beyond the simple subject.

complex sentence—A sentence with a dependent clause and an independent clause. If the dependent clause comes first, the clauses should be separated by a comma.

compound-complex sentence—A sentence with at least two independent clauses and at least one dependent clause.

compound sentence—A sentence with two or more independent clauses.

compound subject—Two or more individual subjects acting together.

conjunction—A word that connects, or joins together, parts of a sentence.

coordinating conjunction—A conjunction such as *and*, *or*, or *but* that is used to join together items of equal rank or importance within the sentence.

correlative conjunction—A coordinating conjunction pair such as *either / or, neither / nor*, and *not only / but also*.

declarative sentence—An ordinary statement that ends with a period.

dependent clause—A group of words that has a subject and a predicate but does not communicate a complete thought all by itself. It cannot stand alone as a complete sentence; its meaning depends on the rest of the sentence.

direct object—A noun or pronoun that identifies a person, place, or thing to which an action is done.

exclamatory sentence—A sentence that expresses strong feeling and ends with an exclamation point.

gender—The quality of a noun or pronoun that has to do with whether the person, place, or thing named is masculine, feminine, or neuter (no gender). Gender is important for pronoun-antedecent agreement.

imperative sentence—A sentence that gives a command; it may end with either a period or an exclamation point. Since the subject of an imperative sentence is understood to be "you," it may be left out.

incomplete sentence—A word, phrase, or dependent clause written as if it were a complete sentence; also called a *sentence fragment*.

independent clause—A group of words that has a subject and a predicate and expresses a complete thought. It can stand alone to form a complete sentence.

indirect object—A noun or pronoun that identifies a person, place, or thing for which an action is done.

interjection—An "extra" word or phrase used to express strong feeling.

interrogative sentence—A sentence that asks a question and ends with a question mark.

noun—A word used to name or identify a person, place, or thing.

number—The quality of a noun or pronoun that has to do with whether the person, place, or thing named is singular (involving only one) or plural (involving more than one). Number is important for pronoun-antedecent agreement and for subject-verb agreement.

object of a preposition—A noun or pronoun that follows a preposition and is being described in relationship to some other part of the sentence.

parts of speech—The different types of words in grammar; each type serves a different purpose. The main parts of speech include nouns, pronouns, verbs, adjectives, adverbs, prepositions, conjunctions, and interjections.

person—The quality of a noun or pronoun that has to do with who is speaking about whom or what. In first person, the subject speaks or writes about him- or herself; in second person, the subject speaks or writes directly to someone else; in third person, the subject speaks or writes to someone else about another person or thing. Person is important for pronoun-antecedent agreement and subject-verb agreement.

phrase—A group of words that work together but do not form a complete sentence. A phrase lacks a subject, a predicate, or both.

preposition—A word such as *around*, *of*, or *with* that helps describe the relationship between a particular noun or pronoun and the rest of the sentence.

prepositional phrase—A group of words that includes a preposition, a noun or pronoun that is considered the object of the preposition, and all related modifiers.

pronoun—A word such as *he, them,* or *whom* that can be used in place of a noun; it should agree with the noun in gender, number, and person.

pronoun-antecedent agreement—Making sure a pronoun matches its antecedent in number, gender, and person.

proofreading—Reading through something in order to find and correct mistakes.

run-on sentence—Two or more independent clauses that are not connected properly.

sentence fragment—See *incomplete sentence.*

simple predicate—A verb identifying the main action or state of being in the sentence.

simple sentence—The most basic kind of complete sentence, with only one complete subject and one complete predicate.

simple subject—A noun or pronoun identifying the person, place, or thing that performs the main action or experiencing the main state of being in the sentence.

subject—A noun or pronoun identifying a person, place, or thing that performs an action or experiences a state of being in the sentence.

subject-verb agreement—Making sure the verb matches the subject in number and person.

subordinating conjunction—A word such as *although, because,* or *while* that introduces a dependent clause.

superlative—The form of an adjective or adverb that shows that something has the greatest or the least amount of a particular quality compared to the other items in question.

tense—The quality of a verb that has to do with when it is being performed or experienced, such as past, present, or future.

verb—A word that identifies an action or state of being.

Further Reading

Books

Kesselman-Turkel, Judi, and Franklynn Peterson. *The Grammar Crammer: How to Write Perfect Sentences.* Madison, Wis.: University of Wisconsin Press, 2003.

Mulvey, Dan. *Grammar the Easy Way.* Hauppauge, N.Y.: Barron's, 2002.

O'Connor, Patricia T. *Woe Is I: The Grammarphobe's Guide to Better English in Plain English,* 2nd ed. New York: The Penguin Publishing Group (Riverhead Books), 2003.

Terban, Marvin. *Checking Your Grammar.* New York: Scholastic, 1994.

Venolia, Jan. *Kids Write Right! What You Need to Be a Writing Powerhouse.* Madison, Wis.: Turtleback Books, 2000.

Internet Addresses

Dr. Grammar

<http://www.drgrammar.org>

Professor James HiDuke—also known as "Dr. Grammar"—is no longer here to answer users' new grammar questions, but his site is full of great info for writers. "Frequently Asked Questions," "Grammar Resources," and "A Writer's Resources" are good places to start.

English Usage, Style and Composition

<http://www.bartleby.com/usage>

This page links users to free online versions of many well-known guides to grammar and usage.

Guide to Grammar and Writing

<http://www.ccc.commnet.edu/grammar/>

Drop-down menus help organize the information on this site, from words and sentences to paragraphs and more. An "Ask Grammar" form allows users to receive e-mail answers to their own tricky grammar questions within just a few days.

Index